WHALE

VS.

GIANT SQUID

BY
JERRY PALLOTTA

ILLUSTRATED BY
ROB BOLSTER

Scholastic Inc.
New York   Toronto   London   Auckland
Sydney   Mexico City   New Delhi   Hong Kong

The publisher would like to thank the following for their
kind permission to use their photographs in this book:

Page 12: bottom: © Dirk Renckhoff / Alamy; page 16: middle: © AKG Images;
bottom: © Mary Evans Picture Library; page 17: © Shutterstock;
page 19: © Louise Murray / Photo Researchers, Inc.; page 24: © The Bridgeman Art Library

This book is for Connie Ross, a New Hampshire reading legend.
—J.P.
This book is dedicated to Edward Hopper.
—R.B.

ISBN 978-0-545-30173-2

Text copyright © 2012 by Jerry Pallotta.
Illustrations copyright © 2012 by Rob Bolster.
All rights reserved. Published by Scholastic Inc.
SCHOLASTIC and associated logos are trademarks and/or registered trademarks of
Scholastic Inc. WHO WOULD WIN? is a registered trademark of Jerry Pallotta.

39 38 37   18/0

Printed in the U.S.A.   40
First printing, September 2012

What would happen if a whale swam near a giant squid? They are both carnivores, or meat eaters. What if they had a fight? Who do you think would win?

SCIENTIFIC NAME OF
SPERM WHALE:
"Physeter macrocephalus"

Meet the sperm whale.

> **BIG FACT**
> *The blue whale is the largest animal on Earth.*

> **COLORFUL FACT**
> *Whales have red blood.*

> **RUNNER-UP FACT**
> *The sperm whale can grow to be 60 feet long and weigh 50 tons.*

It is one of the world's largest whales. All of the biggest whales are baleen whales, which means they have no teeth. The sperm whale is unusual. It is a big whale that has teeth, but only on its bottom jaw.

4

This whale looks like a big head with a tail. Its scientific name means "blower with a big head." It is the largest of all toothed whales. The sperm whale has the largest head of any animal that has ever lived on Earth.

DID YOU KNOW?

The sperm whale has a blowhole at the front of its head.

LONG FACT
Its head can be 20 feet long.

SCIENTIFIC NAME OF GIANT SQUID: "Architeuthis dux"

Meet the giant squid.

> **FACT**
> *Squid, octopuses, nautiluses, and cuttlefish are cephalopods.*

> **BONUS FACT**
> *On restaurant menus, squid is often listed by its Italian name, "calamari."*

A giant squid is a mollusk. A squid belongs to a group of mollusks called cephalopods. *Cephalopod* means "head foot." A squid looks like a head attached to legs. It has eight legs and two extra feeder arms. The legs have suction cups. The feeder arms have hooks and suction cups on the ends that act like hands.

The giant squid has fins for steering. It propels itself by sucking water into its head and squeezing the water out. A squid works the same way as a jet engine.

A giant squid can be 60 feet long and weigh 450 pounds. Most giant squid that have washed up on beaches are 20 to 30 feet long. That's a lot of calamari!

MAMMALS

Whales are mammals. The people reading this book are mammals, too. Here are some other mammals:

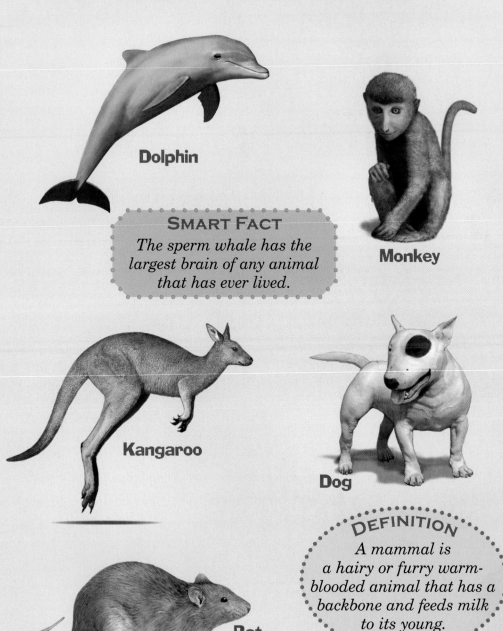

Dolphin

Monkey

SMART FACT
The sperm whale has the largest brain of any animal that has ever lived.

Kangaroo

Dog

Rat

DEFINITION
A mammal is a hairy or furry warm-blooded animal that has a backbone and feeds milk to its young.

MOLLUSKS

Squid are mollusks. Here are examples of other mollusks:

Mussel

Octopus

Clam

Snail

Cuttlefish

DEFINITION
A mollusk is a soft-bodied animal that usually lives in water and has a protective shell.

EYES

The eye of a sperm whale is only about two inches wide.

FUN FACT

A sperm whale can dive down half a mile. There is hardly any light at that depth.

EYES

Here is a human eyeball.

Here is a giant squid eyeball in comparison. The giant squid eyeball is the largest eyeball in the world. It is as big as a basketball. Its giant eyeballs allow the squid to see at great depths.

TEETH

The sperm whale has long teeth. The teeth are shaped like sidewalk chalk. Notice that it has no teeth on its upper jaw. When a sperm whale closes its mouth, its bottom teeth fit into the indentations in its upper jaw.

FUN FACT
A sperm whale has 20 to 25 teeth on each side of its lower jaw.

BONUS FACT
You can tell how old a sperm whale is by the layers in its teeth.

DID YOU KNOW?
Whalers used to carve beautiful designs on whale teeth and whale bone. This type of art is called scrimshaw.

BEAK

Between its eight legs and its two feeder arms is the squid's mouth. It does not have teeth. Squid have a beak. It looks like a parrot's beak.

FACT
The tip of a squid's beak is hard and tough, but the lower end is more rubbery.

The beak is made of chitin, a material which is like

TAILS

The tail of a sperm whale can be 16 feet across. Whales have horizontal tails.

> **DID YOU KNOW?**
> *The winglike tail is also called a fluke.*

> **TRY THIS**
> *Use a measuring tape to mark 16 feet across your classroom. Wow! That is a wide fluke!*

Other fluke shapes:

blue whale

humpback whale

sei whale

right whale

FINS

The body of a giant squid is called the mantle or torso.
At one end are fins. The giant squid can use its fins to steer.
It can also reverse the motion of its fins to swim backward.

FACT
*People have seen giant
squid jump completely out
of the water.*

FUN FACT
Squid have three hearts.
♥ ♥ ♥

BONUS FACT
*The squid can also steer
itself with its legs.*

OIL

Sad but true: Before the discovery of petroleum, whales were a source of oil. It is estimated that 600,000 sperm whales were killed for their oil.

FACT
There are 6 to 8 barrels of oil in the head of a sperm whale.

BONUS FACT
The first time a whale was killed for oil was in 1690. The busiest whaling years were in the 1700s and 1800s.

This is what a typical Nantucket whaling ship looked like. They would often leave port and return four years later.

If whalers harpooned a whale and the whale took off, it was called a Nantucket sleighride.

CASH REWARD

No one has ever caught a giant squid and kept it alive. If you ever catch one, it may be worth $1,000,000. Someone will be willing to pay it.

$1,000,000
AWARD

DINNER

Sperm whales eat giant squid, squid, sting rays, octopuses, and fish.

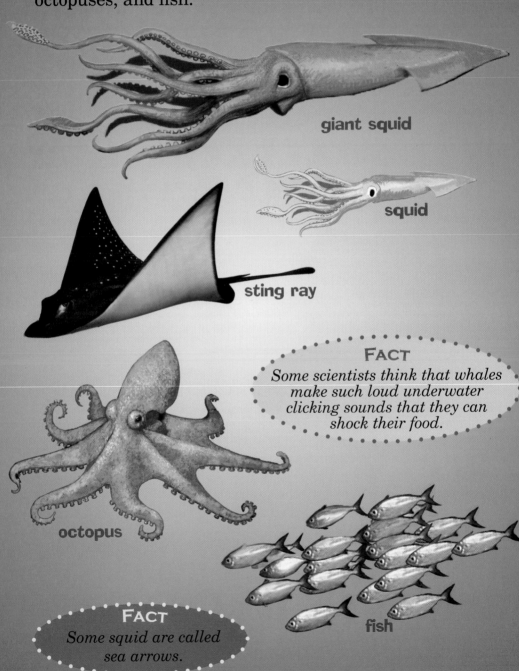

giant squid

squid

sting ray

FACT

Some scientists think that whales make such loud underwater clicking sounds that they can shock their food.

octopus

fish

FACT

Some squid are called sea arrows.

SUPPER

Giant squid eat fish, shrimps, and other squid. They grab food with their long feeder arms. The feeder arms have sharp spines on the ends. They pull the food into their beaks.

FACT
Squid arms and legs are also called tentacles.

close-up of a feeder arm

COLORFUL FACT
Giant squid have blue blood.

SPEED

A sperm whale can swim 25 miles per hour.

SPEED LIMIT 25

DEPTH

1/2 MILE

A sperm whale can dive half a mile deep.

sperm whale

Empire State Building

ocean floor

SPEED

A giant squid can swim 20 miles per hour.

SPEED LIMIT 20

ocean floor

underwater canyon

DEPTH ?

It is not known how far a giant squid can dive.
It can dive deeper than a whale. A giant squid is
more agile than a whale. It can change direction
suddenly and can swim backward.

FACT
*Squid do not need to
come up for air.*

21

ECHOLOCATION

In deep water, the whale relies on echolocation to find its way around. It finds its food by bouncing sound signals off its prey. The whale is lucky compared to a squid. A giant squid cannot hear.

DEFINITION

Bouncing sound back from its prey is called echolocation. The whale uses this to learn where its food is.

SOUND FACT

Sonar is the location of objects through sound waves. Bats, whales, shrews, and some birds have sonar. Submarines have sonar, too!

There are many things we don't know about the sperm whale. We don't know why they do not have teeth in their top jaw. We do not know how many get killed by giant squid.

INK

We don't know how long a giant squid lives. Some scientists think it is only three years.

SECRET WEAPON
Squid blow black ink at their attackers. This is called billowing.

DINNER FACT
Some famous chefs use squid ink to make black pasta. It is called squid-ink pasta.

We don't know how deep they can dive. We don't know how many there are. We don't know where they live, but it appears they prefer deep, colder water. We don't know why no one has been able to catch one alive.

DID YOU KNOW?
There are no known freshwater squid.

FAMOUS WHALE

Moby-Dick is a famous American novel written by Herman Melville. The whale in the story is a giant albino sperm whale. Moby Dick bit the leg off a captain, who vowed revenge. At the end, the whale rams and sinks the ship.

FUN FACT
Moby-Dick *also became a famous movie.*

The story was based on a real sperm whale that rammed and sank the Nantucket whale ship *Essex*. A nonfiction book was written about the event, called *In the Heart of the Sea* by Nathaniel Philbrick.

FAMOUS LEGEND

For hundreds of years, sailors around the world have been afraid of giant squid. A legend is that they come out of the deep and are so large they can swallow a ship.

SCHOLASTIC CLASSICS

20,000 Leagues Under the Sea

...Verne

With an introduction by Bruce Coville

SCHOLASTIC

Science fiction writer Jules Verne wrote about a giant squid attacking a submarine in a novel called
20,000 Leagues Under the Sea

The whale dives. It is looking for food. It sends out sound waves, hoping to find a tasty meal. It senses a few small fish. The whale is hungry. It is looking for a nice giant calamari dinner.

A giant squid is in deep water and out of range.

The giant squid decides to move to shallower water, an easier place to find food. Most fish and squid live in water less than 200 feet deep.

The whale senses the giant squid a quarter of a mile deep. It dives deeper.

The giant squid doesn't notice the whale right away. The whale clicks a few sounds, locates the giant squid, then attacks with its mouth open. The whale grabs a small piece of one of the squid's arms.

The giant squid blows ink in the whale's face, then darts away.

The whale swims after the giant squid. The squid sees the whale and decides to attack first. The squid realizes it is in for a fight. It puts all its legs and feeder arms on the whale. Suction cups and hooks scrape the whale's skin.

The squid tries to hold the whale down until the whale runs out of air. Its plan doesn't work.

The whale maneuvers and bites a chunk of the squid and a few of the squid's arms. A few more bites and the giant squid is in deep trouble.

The whale thinks the giant squid is delicious.

The whale wins, but he has sucker and scratch marks all over his head. That fight hurt!

WHO HAS THE ADVANTAGE? CHECKLIST

WHALE

☐ Length
☐ Weight
☐ Brain
☐ Eyes
☐ Teeth
☐ Weapons
☐ Speed

GIANT SQUID

☐
☐
☐
☐
☐
☐
☐

Author note: This is one way the fight might have ended.
How would you write the ending?